VENUS

PLANETS IN OUR SOLAR SYSTEM

CHILDREN'S ASTRONOMY EDITION

Speedy Publishing LLC
40 E. Main St. #1156
Newark, DE 19711
www.speedypublishing.com

Copyright 2015

Venus is called after the Roman Goddess of love and beauty.

Venus is the second planet from the Sun, orbiting every 224.7 Earth days.

Venus is the brightest planet in the Solar System and can be seen even in daylight if you know where to look.

The
atmosphere
of Venus
made up
mainly of
carbon
dioxide.

Venus is surrounded by clouds. The clouds are so thick that little light reaches the surface.

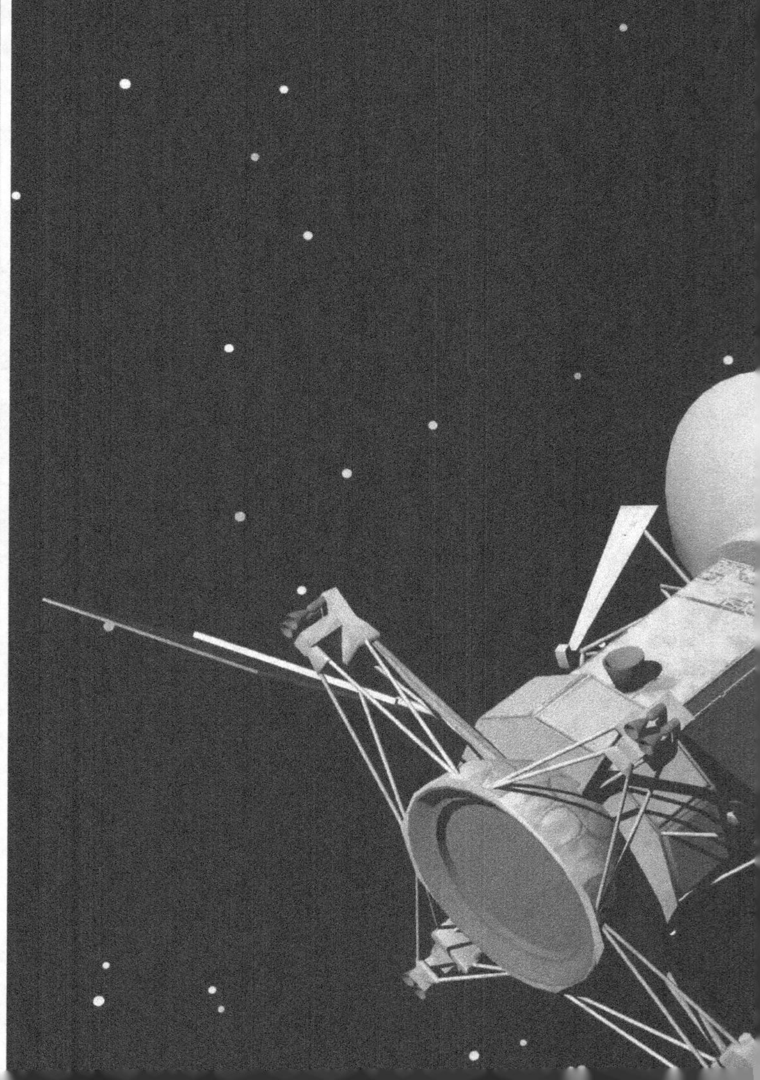

Venus is very similar to Earth in size and mass. It is sometimes called Earth's sister planet.

The surface
of Venus is
a stormy
desert full
of many
craters and
very active
volcanoes.

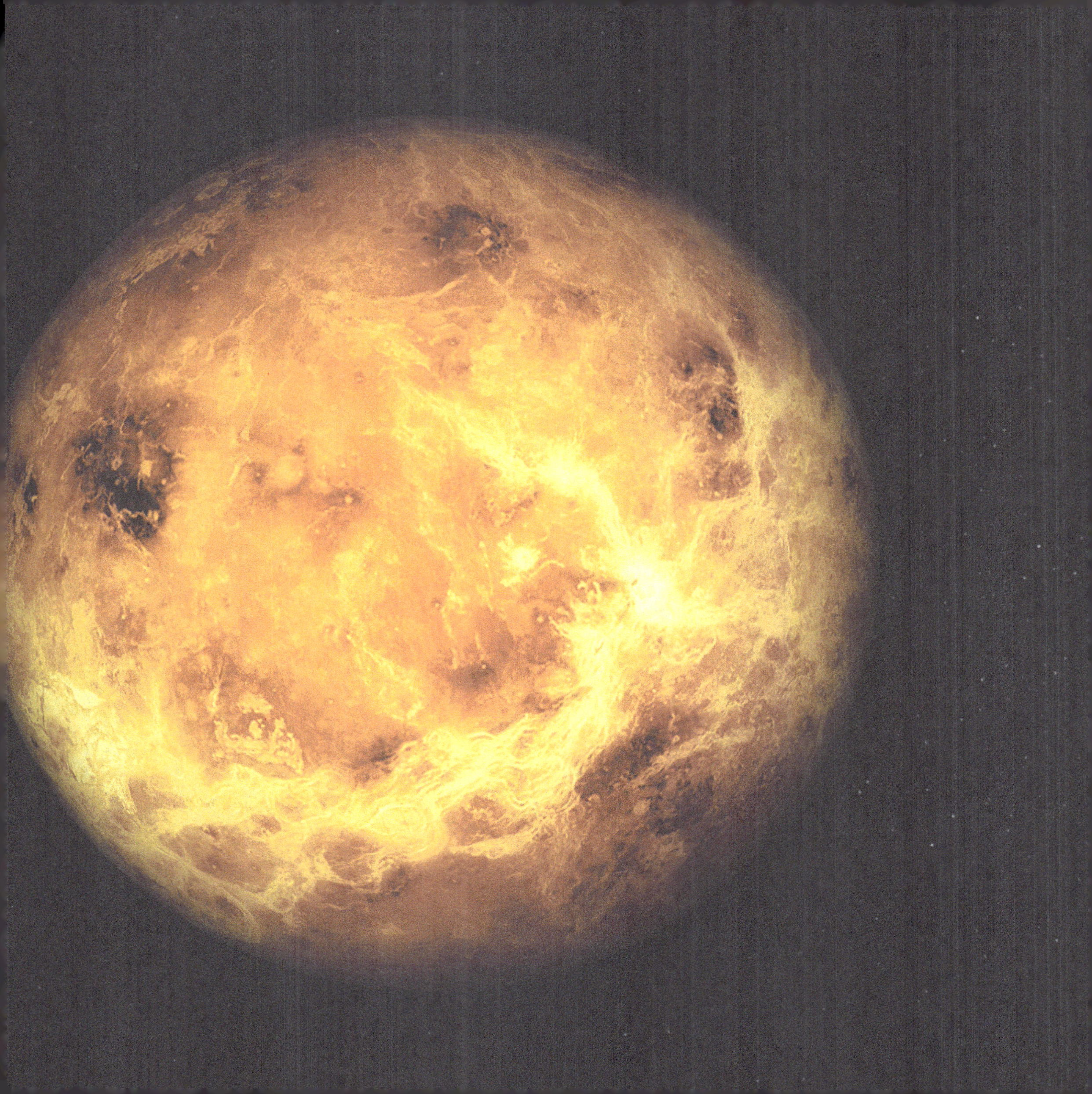

There are over 100 giant volcanoes on Venus.

Venus is the hottest planet in our solar system. The temperature on the surface of Venus is about 860° Fahrenheit.

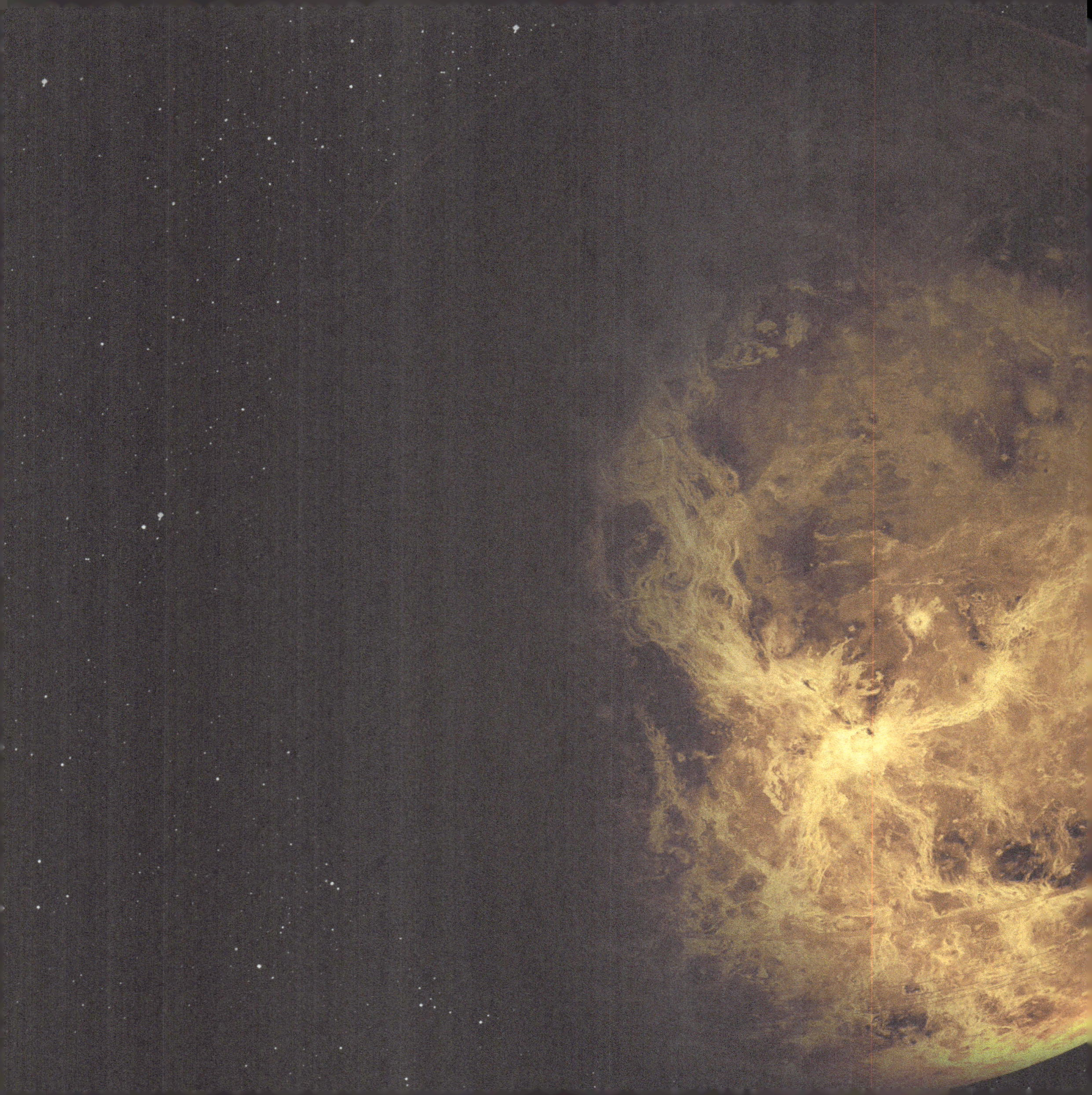

The circumference of Venus is 12,103 kilometres.

Venus has
no natural
satellite.

Venus is 67 million miles away from the Sun.

The largest continent on Venus has been named Aphrodite.

Venus rotates backwards from the way the rest of the planets rotate.

Venus is also
known as
the Morning
Star and the
Evening Star.

Because of Venus's hot atmosphere, all the probes that have landed have been destroyed within a few hours.

Venus is the
closest planet
to Earth.

Venus rotates very slowly - one day on Venus is equivalent to 243 Earth days.

The first
person to
witness the
phases of
Venus was
Galileo Galilei.